About the Book

What would it be like to live in a desert? For us, the hot, dry sand and rocks would make an uncomfortable home. But there are some plants and animals that have learned to live together and thrive in arid desert lands.

Simply and vividly, the author tells about these plants and animals—how they get food and water, where they live, and how they protect themselves. Some, like the cactus and the kangaroo rat, manufacture or store their own water. Some have learned to rely on other plants and animals for their necessities. All are at home in the desert because over the centuries each species has slowly evolved in order to survive in the unique environment of the desert.

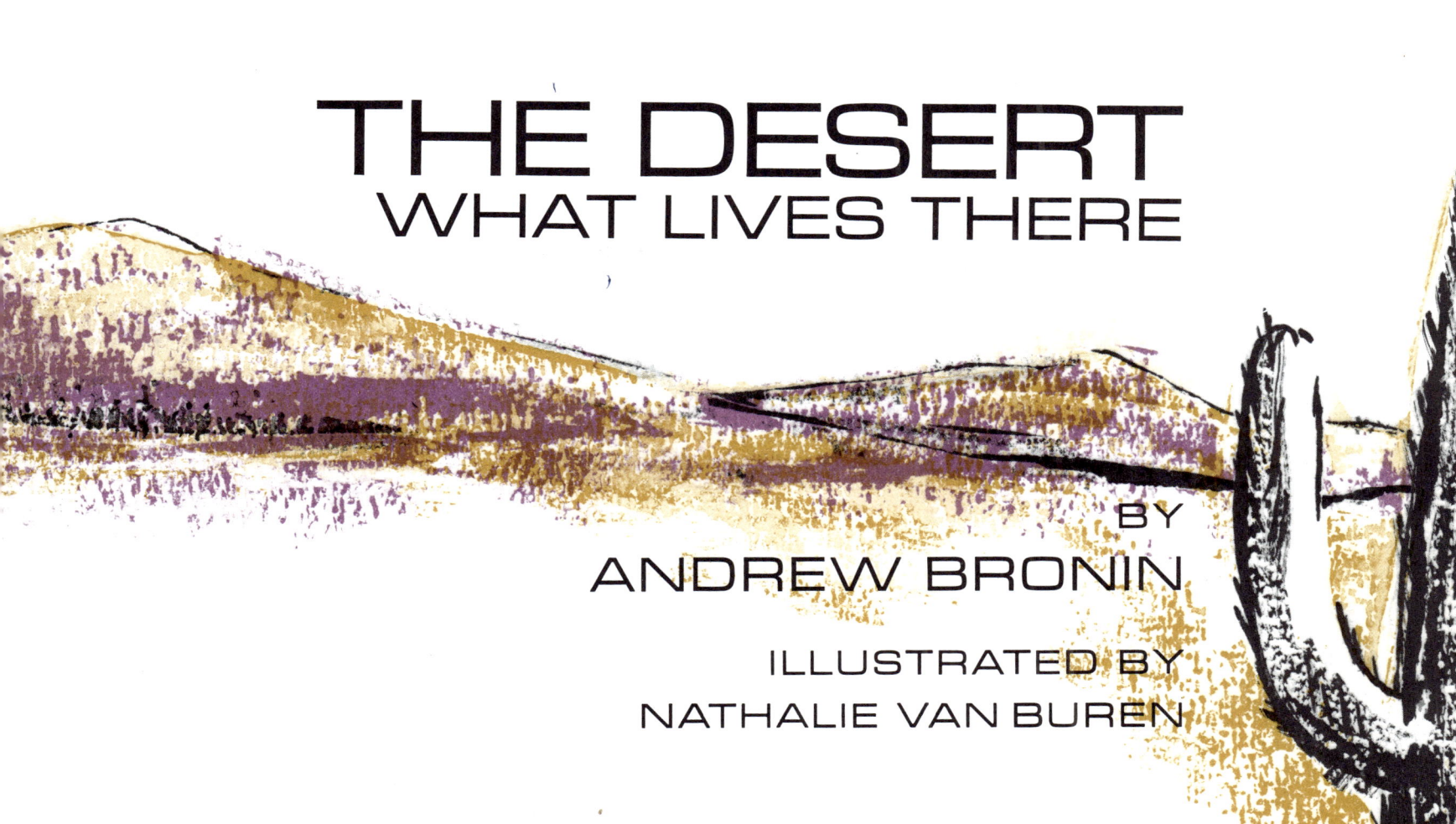

THE DESERT
WHAT LIVES THERE

BY
ANDREW BRONIN

ILLUSTRATED BY
NATHALIE VAN BUREN

COWARD, McCANN & GEOGHEGAN, INC.
NEW YORK

Text copyright © 1972 by Andrew Bronin
Illustrations copyright © 1972 by Nathalie van Buren
All rights reserved. This book, or parts thereof, may not be reproduced in any form without permission in writing from the publishers. Published simultaneously in Canada by Longmans Canada Limited, Toronto.
SBN: GB-698-30440-3
SBN: TR-698-20197-3
Library of Congress Catalog Card Number: 72-76694
PRINTED IN THE UNITED STATES OF AMERICA
07211

*For Joseph Bronin,
Milton Hoffman,
Myron Bronin
and Xidi.*

The desert is a land of rock and sand. Rain falls only once or twice a year in the desert. The sun beats down, and the sand and rocks grow hot and dry.

Who is at home in the desert? Could the plants or animals near your house live there? Could you? Every living thing needs a home that provides food, shelter, and protection. Some plants and animals have learned to get along together and make their homes in the dry, sandy desert.

The cactus plant is at home in the desert. The cactus plant has a special way of getting water in the dry desert soil. It spreads its roots out close to the surface of the ground. When rain comes, the roots soak up all the water they can. The roots of most plants go down, not out. Do you think they would be at home in the desert?

Once a cactus plant gets water, it saves the water for the dry days ahead. The prickly pear cactus stores its water in many tiny pads that grow on its branches. The barrel cactus stores water in its "barrel" stem. A cactus stores up enough water in one rainstorm to last it a whole year. The desert may be dry, but inside its stem, a cactus is like a juicy apple.

The desert tortoise is at home in the desert. He stores water, too. Have you ever filled a plastic bag with water? The tortoise has "bags" full of water inside him. They are called water sacs. When it rains, the tortoise drinks all the water he can. Then he stores the water in his water sacs. He can live for months without taking another drink.

The kangaroo rat is at home in the dry, waterless desert. The kangaroo rat makes his own water. If you were a scientist, you could take certain ingredients and make water. The kangaroo rat isn't a scientist—but his body makes water from dry seeds. He eats the seeds, and from the seeds, he has his ingredients. The ingredients become water inside the rat. The kangaroo rat never takes a drink of water in his life. He doesn't have to: He makes his own.

The cactus, the tortoise, and the kangaroo rat are at home in the desert because they know how to get water. But water isn't the only thing that makes plants and animals able to live in the desert. They also need protection.

The kangaroo rat can protect himself. When a snake or a fox tries to catch him, he jumps high in the air, like a kangaroo. At the same time, he kicks sand backward into his enemy's face. All the snake or the fox gets is a mouthful of sand.